MW01102062

T A K E   I T   A P A R T

DIGGER

By Chris Oxlade

Illustrated by Mike Grey

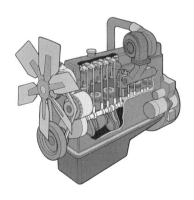

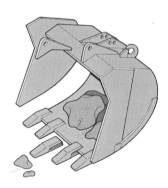

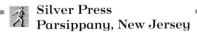

Silver Press
Parsippany, New Jersey

First published in the U.K. in 1996 by

Belitha Press Limited, London House,
Great Eastern Wharf, Parkgate Road, London SW11 4NQ

Printed in China.

Editor: Mary-Jane Wilkins
Designer: Guy Callaby
Illustrator: Mike Grey
Consultants: David Wheeler
and Elizabeth Atkinson

Published in the United States in 1997 by

Silver Press
A Division of Simon & Schuster
299 Jefferson Road
Parsippany, New Jersey 07054

Library of Congress Cataloging-in-Publication Data
Oxlade, Chris
Digger/by Chris Oxlade.
p.   cm. (Take it apart)
Reprint. Originally published: London, England: Belitha Press Limited, 1996.
Includes index.

Summary: Describes the parts of a backhoe and how they work.
1. Backhoes–Parts–Juvenile literature. 2. Machine parts–Juvenile
literature. [1. Backhoes. 2. Machinery.] I.Title. II. Series.
TA735.094 1997 96-27529
629.225–dc20   CIP   AC

ISBN 0-382-39671-5 (LSB) 10 9 8 7 6 5 4 3 2 1
ISBN 0-382-39672-3 (PBK) 10 9 8 7 6 5 4 3 2 1

Inside This Book

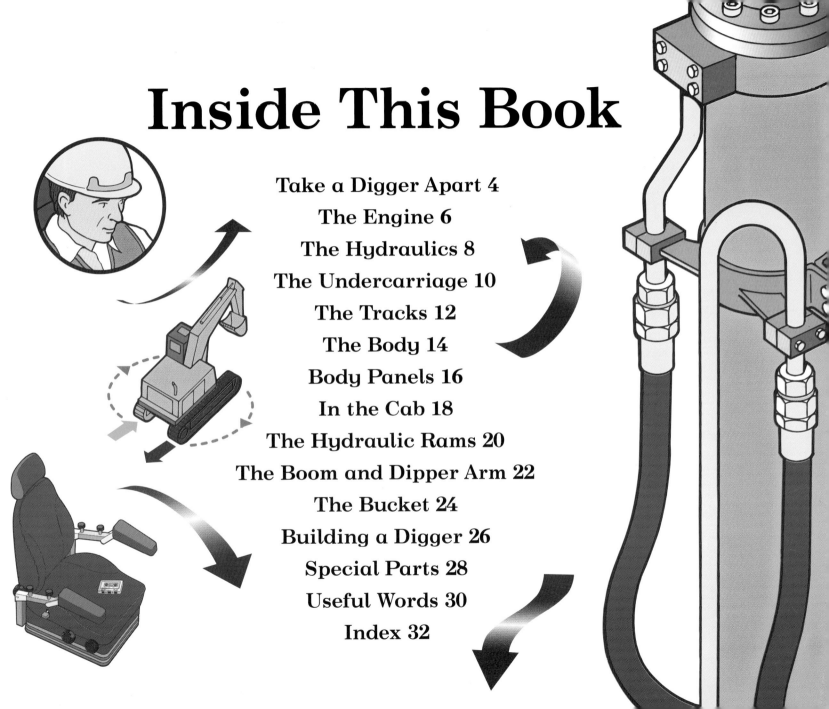

Take a Digger Apart

● A digger is made of thousands of parts.

● The parts are made of metal, plastic, glass, and other materials.

● The parts are put together in a factory.

● This book shows you the main parts of a digger and how they fit together.

Fact Box
The digger here is called a backhoe excavator. It digs up earth and rock. It is used to dig rock out of quarries or to make new roads.

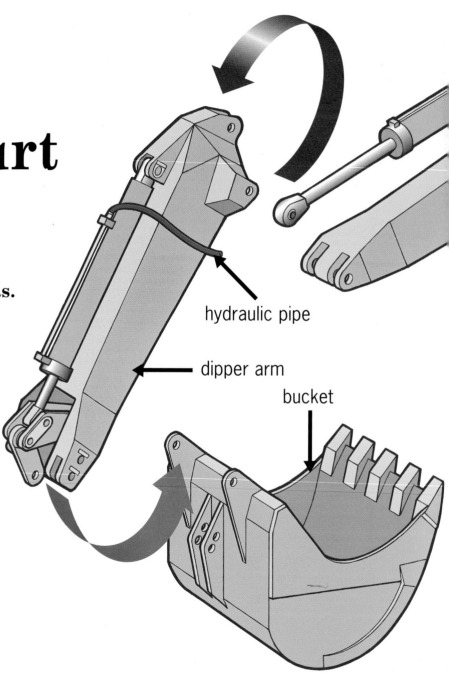

hydraulic pipe

dipper arm

bucket

4

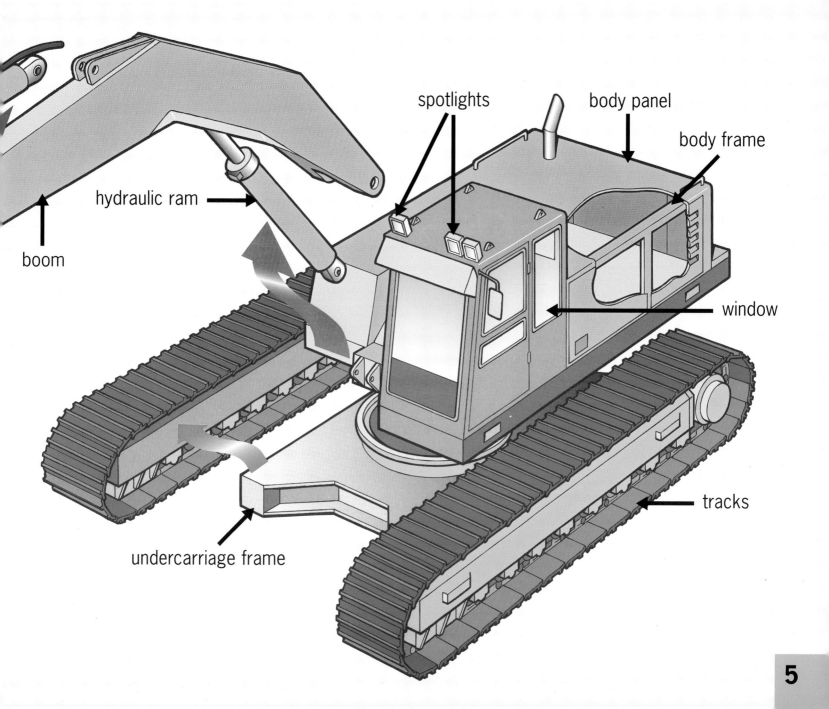

spotlights

body panel

body frame

hydraulic ram

boom

window

undercarriage frame

tracks

5

The Engine

🔩 The engine makes the power that the digger needs to work.

🔩 The power makes the tracks go around, the body swing around, and the boom go up and down.

🔩 The engine needs diesel fuel to make it work.

🔩 Inside the engine are chambers called cylinders. Inside each cylinder is a piston, which moves up and down.

Fact Box
The diesel engine in this digger is five times bigger than the engine in a family car. It is about three times as powerful as a car engine.

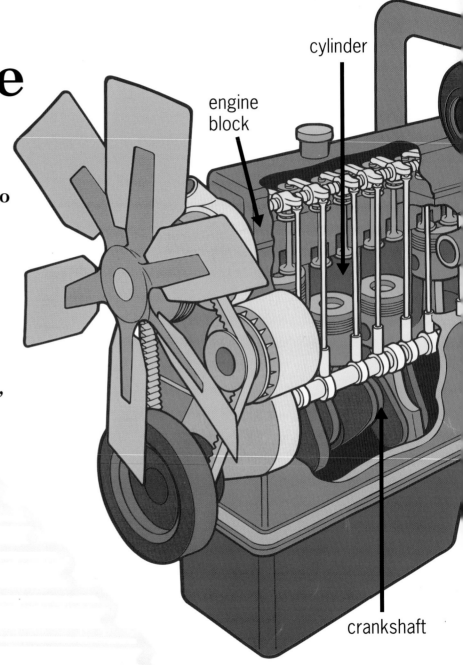

cylinder

engine block

crankshaft

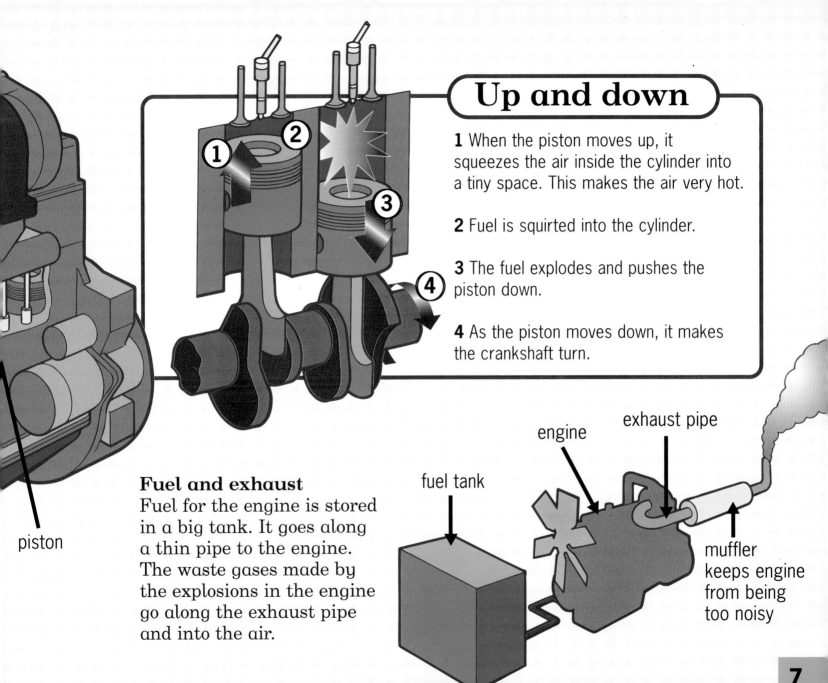

Up and down

1 When the piston moves up, it squeezes the air inside the cylinder into a tiny space. This makes the air very hot.

2 Fuel is squirted into the cylinder.

3 The fuel explodes and pushes the piston down.

4 As the piston moves down, it makes the crankshaft turn.

piston

Fuel and exhaust

Fuel for the engine is stored in a big tank. It goes along a thin pipe to the engine. The waste gases made by the explosions in the engine go along the exhaust pipe and into the air.

fuel tank

engine

exhaust pipe

muffler keeps engine from being too noisy

The Hydraulics

🔩 All the digger's parts are moved by a hydraulic system.

🔩 The hydraulic system is full of liquid called hydraulic fluid.

🔩 The hydraulic fluid is moved along pipes by pumps. The pumps are powered by the digger's engine.

🔩 The moving fluid makes the parts of the digger move.

Fact Box
The hydraulic pumps in this digger can pump nearly 116 gallons of hydraulic fluid every minute. That's enough fluid to fill 14 cans of soda every second.

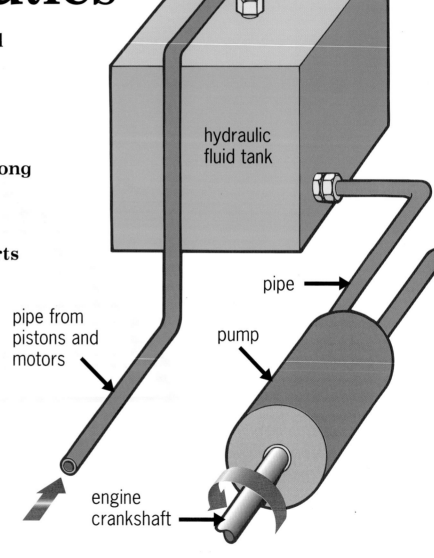

hydraulic fluid tank

pipe from pistons and motors

pipe

pump

engine crankshaft

Hydraulic pipes

The pipes that carry hydraulic fluid around the digger have to be very strong. Otherwise they would burst. Some are flexible and some are rigid. Some of the flexible pipes are protected by metal hoops.

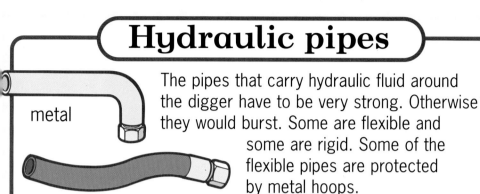

metal

rubber

protected rubber

fluid goes in here

fluid goes out here

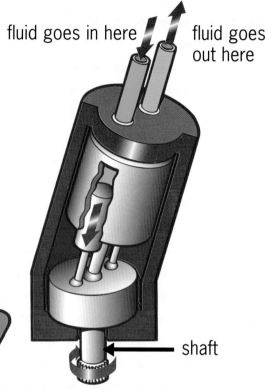

shaft

valves open and close to let fluid go to motors and rams

pipes to pistons and motors

Hydraulic motors
A hydraulic motor works when hydraulic fluid is pumped through it. The motor turns a shaft. In this digger, hydraulic motors make the tracks go around and the body swing from side to side.

The Undercarriage

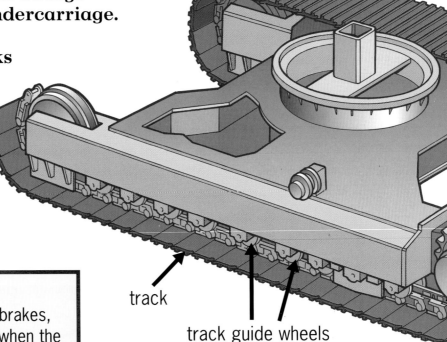

undercarriage frame made from steel plates

- The digger's undercarriage is the part nearest the ground.

- The body of the digger swings around on top of the undercarriage.

- This digger has tracks on its undercarriage.

- Some diggers have wheels instead of tracks.

- The undercarriage makes a strong, stable base for the digger.

Fact Box
Tracked undercarriages have brakes, which come on automatically when the tracks are not moving. This keeps the digger from moving by accident.

track

track guide wheels keep tracks in place

wheel with teeth makes track move

Wheeled undercarriage

Digger wheels are big, with thick tires for moving along on muddy, bumpy ground. They also let the digger drive along the road. The digger has legs called outriggers, which the driver puts down when the digger lifts heavy loads.

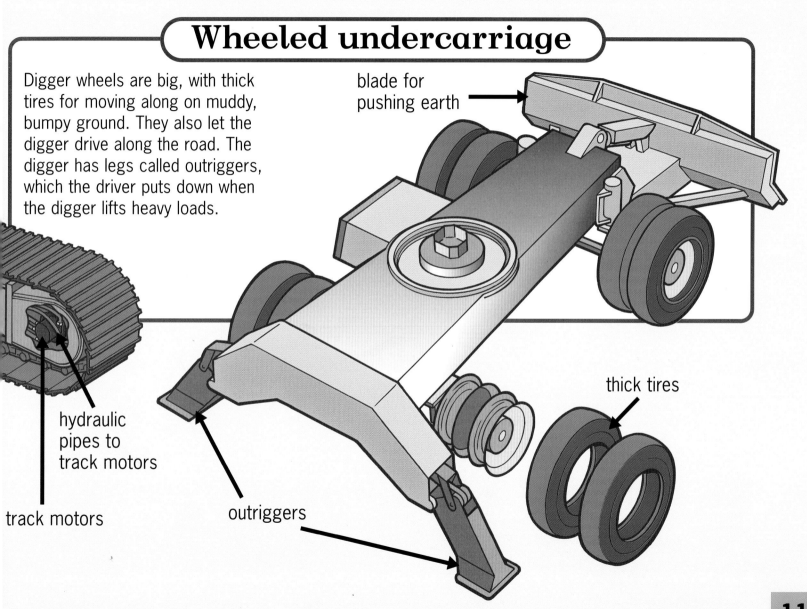

blade for pushing earth

thick tires

hydraulic pipes to track motors

track motors

outriggers

The Tracks

● This digger has wide metal tracks.

● They keep the digger from sinking into muddy ground.

● The tracks are long, floppy loops made from many parts joined together.

● The driver presses pedals in the cab to make the tracks move.

track guide wheels

Fact Box
Diggers with tracks are not very fast. This digger has a top speed of 3 miles per hour. That's about the speed you do when you're walking quickly.

Track guide wheels

The tracks are kept in place by wheels called track guide wheels on the undercarriage frame. There is a big wheel at each end of the track and smaller wheels along it.

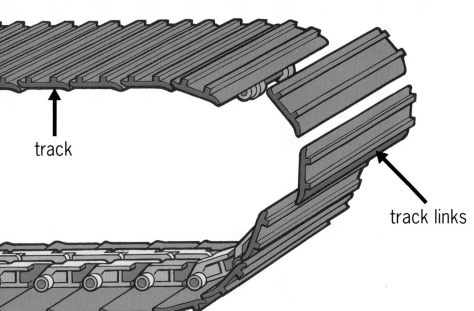

track

track links

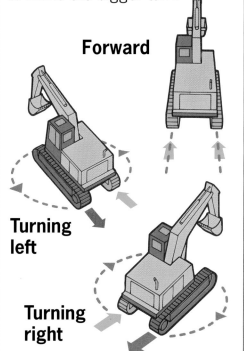

Moving with tracks

The tracks move in the same direction to make the digger go backward or forward. They move in opposite directions to make the digger turn.

Forward

Turning left

Turning right

The Body

🔩 The body is the main part of the digger.

🔩 The frame of the body is like a large metal plate.

🔩 The body sits on top of the undercarriage.

🔩 All the other parts of the digger are attached to the top of the frame.

Fact Box
The digger's body can swing in a circle–all the way around from pointing forward–in ten seconds.

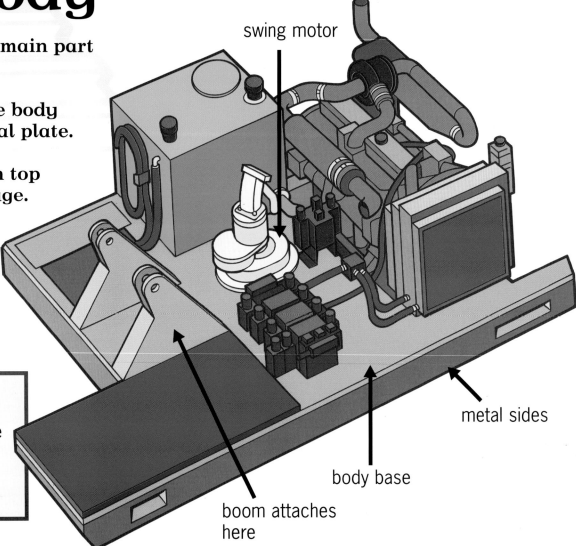

swing motor

metal sides

body base

boom attaches here

Swing motor

The swing motor makes the body swing around on top of the undercarriage. The motor is powered by hydraulic fluid. It turns a gear wheel, which presses against a ring of teeth on the undercarriage.

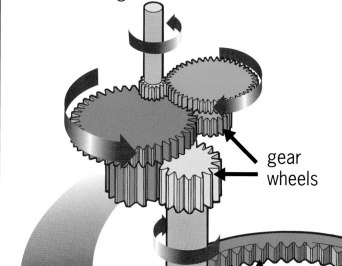

gear wheels

ring of teeth on undercarriage

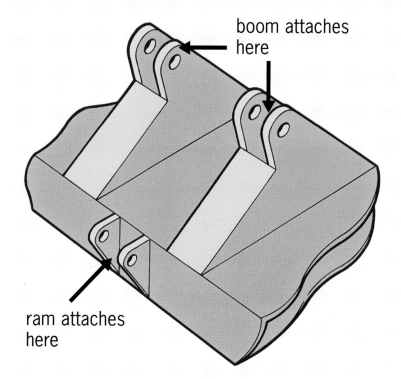

boom attaches here

ram attaches here

Boom attachment

The boom is on the front of the body. There are pieces of metal on the body that fasten to the end of the boom. There is also a piece of metal for the ram that makes the boom move.

Body Panels

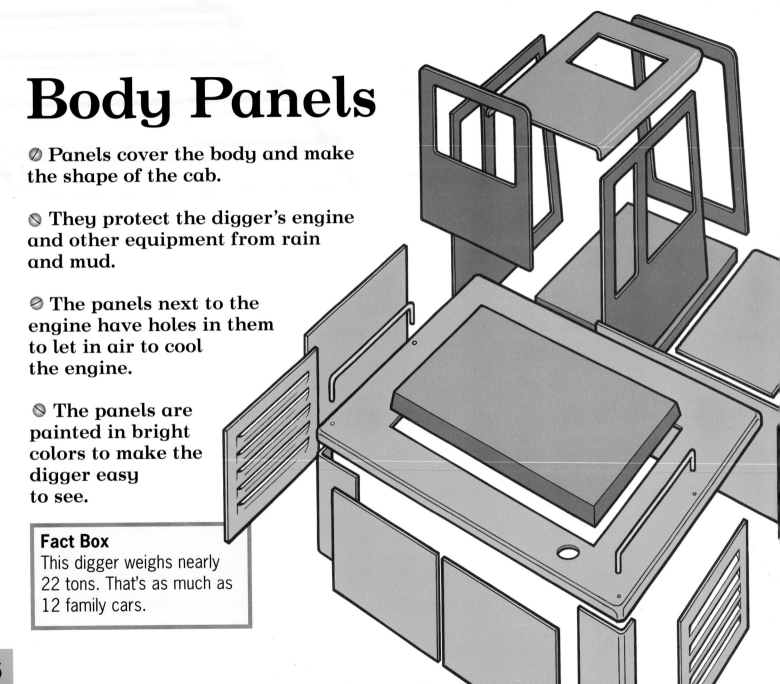

⊘ Panels cover the body and make the shape of the cab.

◐ They protect the digger's engine and other equipment from rain and mud.

⊘ The panels next to the engine have holes in them to let in air to cool the engine.

◐ The panels are painted in bright colors to make the digger easy to see.

Fact Box
This digger weighs nearly 22 tons. That's as much as 12 family cars.

Windows and wipers

There are large windows in the cab so the driver can see all around the digger easily. There is even a small window in the roof. The front window can slide into the roof of the cab.

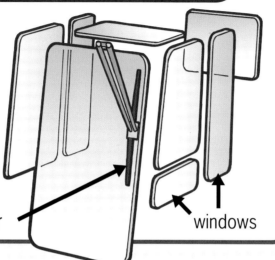

windshield wiper

windows

Lights and mirrors

On top of the cab and the body are powerful spotlights. They light up the ground in front of the digger so the driver can work in the dark. There are also mirrors so that the driver can see behind the digger.

light

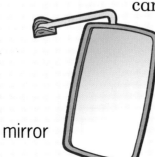

mirror

Cab door

On one side of the cab is a large door, which opens so the driver can climb in and out. Outside the digger, under the door, are steps up to the cab.

In the Cab

🔘 **The driver sits inside the cab.**

🔘 **There are levers and pedals that the driver uses to control the digger.**

🔘 **Panels of dials and lights show the driver whether the digger's equipment is working properly.**

🔘 **A heater and ventilation system makes sure that the driver is not too cold or too hot.**

Fact Box
The cab keeps out the sound of the noisy machinery. There's even a radio-cassette player for the driver to listen to.

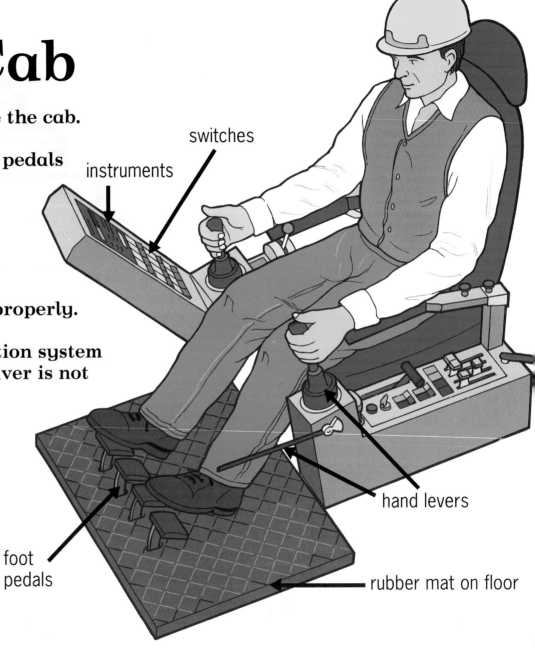

switches

instruments

hand levers

foot pedals

rubber mat on floor

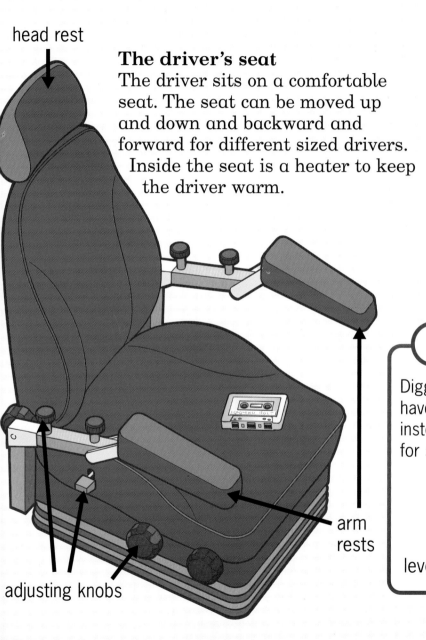

head rest

The driver's seat
The driver sits on a comfortable seat. The seat can be moved up and down and backward and forward for different sized drivers. Inside the seat is a heater to keep the driver warm.

Digging controls
The driver controls the digger with hand levers and foot pedals. The levers make the boom, dipper arm, and bucket move. They also make the body swing around. The pedals make the tracks move.

arm rests

adjusting knobs

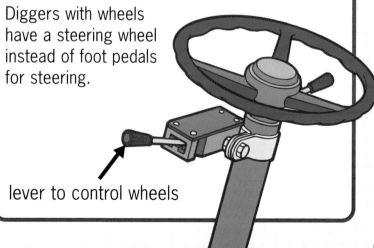

Steering wheel
Diggers with wheels have a steering wheel instead of foot pedals for steering.

lever to control wheels

The Hydraulic Rams

- The digger's boom, dipper arm, and bucket are moved by hydraulic rams.

- Each ram has a cylinder and a piston.

- A cylinder is a narrow tube.

- A piston slides in and out of the cylinder.

- It is pushed in and out by hydraulic fluid.

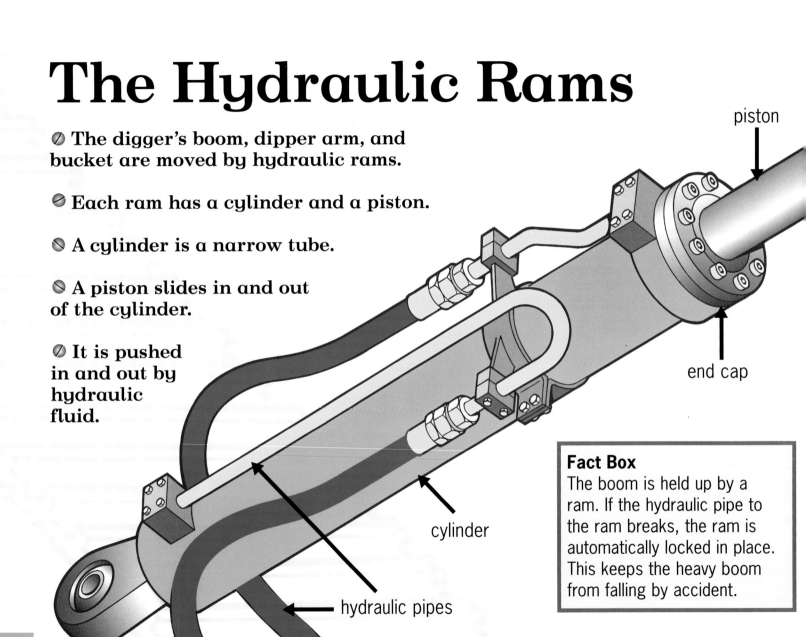

piston

end cap

cylinder

hydraulic pipes

Fact Box
The boom is held up by a ram. If the hydraulic pipe to the ram breaks, the ram is automatically locked in place. This keeps the heavy boom from falling by accident.

eye ring fasten
to digger parts

Hydraulic pipes

The fluid for the rams goes along hydraulic pipes. The pipes come from inside the digger's body. They are attached to the digger with clamps. There are flexible pipes where the boom needs to bend.

How the rams work

A piston moves out of a cylinder when hydraulic fluid is pumped into one end of the cylinder. It moves in when fluid is pumped into the other end of the cylinder.

fluid out here

fluid in here

Piston going out

fluid in here

fluid out here

Piston going in

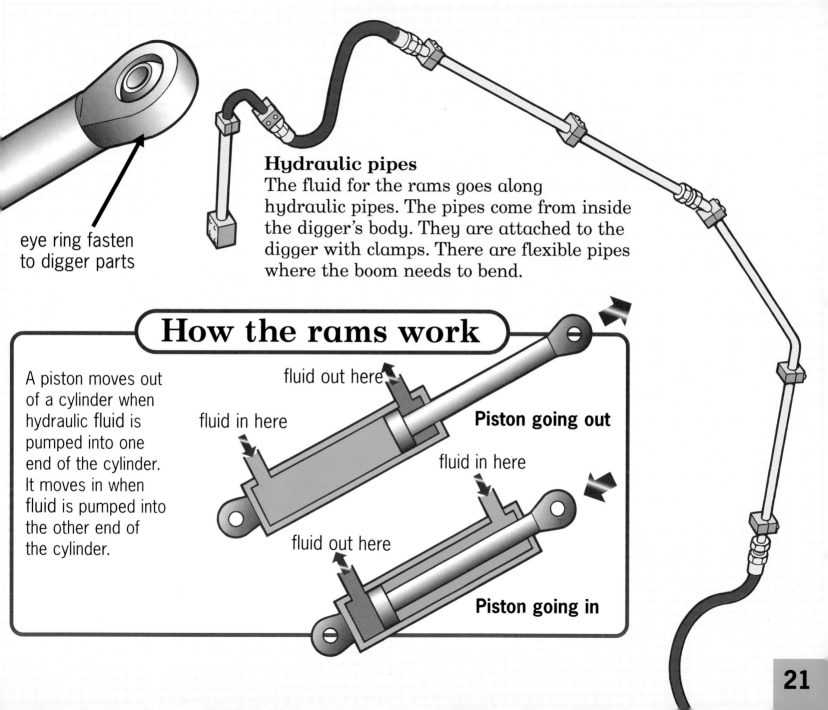

The Boom and Dipper Arm

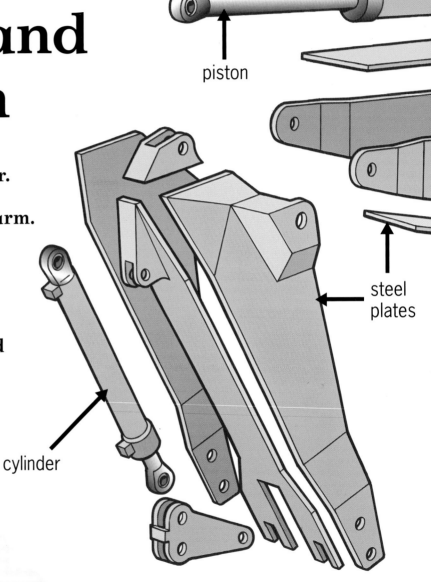

piston

steel plates

cylinder

- The boom is long and thin. It stretches out in front of the digger.

- The boom supports the dipper arm.

- The boom and dipper arm are made from steel plates joined together.

- Rams make the boom go up and down and the dipper arm swing.

Fact Box
Diggers can have extra long booms and dipper arms. They can reach much farther than other diggers. Some can dig a hole 33 feet deep.

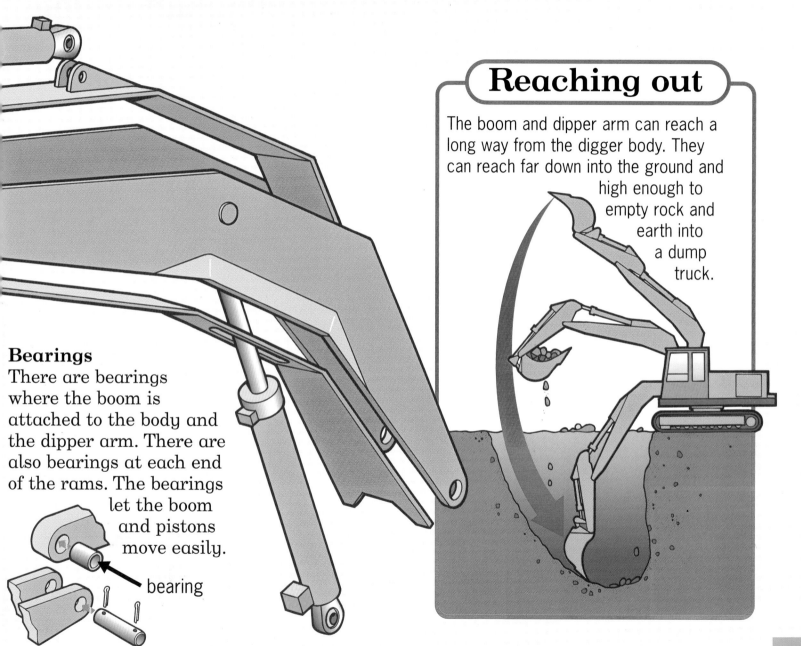

Reaching out

The boom and dipper arm can reach a long way from the digger body. They can reach far down into the ground and high enough to empty rock and earth into a dump truck.

Bearings

There are bearings where the boom is attached to the body and the dipper arm. There are also bearings at each end of the rams. The bearings let the boom and pistons move easily.

bearing

The Bucket

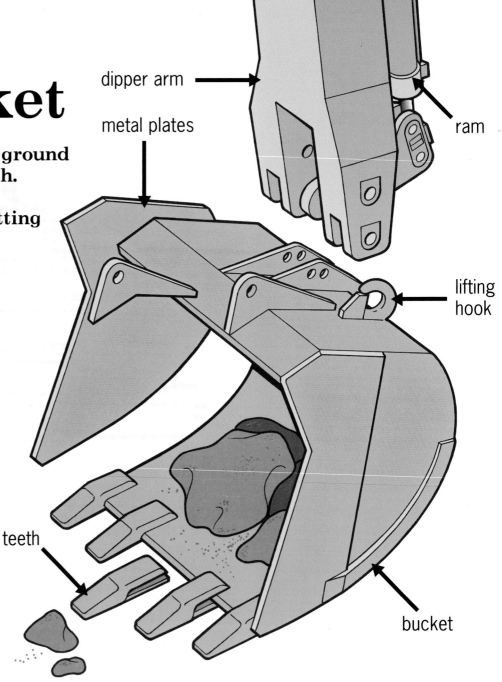

dipper arm

metal plates

ram

⊘ The bucket digs into the ground and picks up rock and earth.

◐ It has sharp teeth for cutting into the ground.

◐ The bucket hangs on the end of the dipper arm.

◐ A ram makes the bucket scoop up rock and earth. It also tips the bucket to empty it.

lifting hook

Fact Box
Digger buckets are very big. A medium-sized bucket holds enough rocks to fill two bathtubs. It would take half an hour to fill with a spade.

teeth

bucket

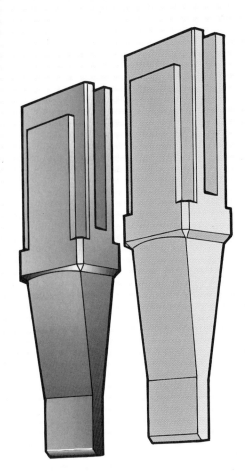

Strong teeth
The bucket's teeth are made of extra-tough steel. The teeth slice into the ground and keep the bucket from being damaged.

Different buckets

Different sized buckets can be put on the digger. Narrow buckets are for digging trenches in the ground. Medium-sized buckets are for digging up rocky ground. Wide buckets are for scooping up sand or gravel to load onto trucks.

medium-sized bucket

narrow bucket

wide bucket

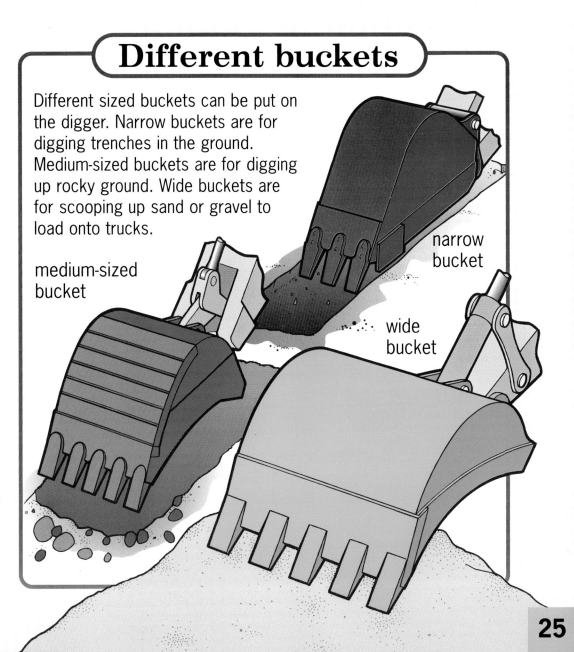

Building a Digger

◉ Diggers are made on a production line in a factory.

◉ Different parts are added as the digger moves along the line.

◉ The main parts of the digger are built first. Then they are joined together.

Fact Box
A computer knows the shapes of all the parts of the digger. It controls the machines that cut them out.

Making the frames
Pieces of steel are cut out and welded together to make the track frame and the body frame.

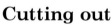

Making the boom
More pieces of steel are cut out and welded together to make the boom and dipper arm.

Cutting out
Steel shapes are cut out with a cutting torch. The torch has a hot and powerful flame, which melts the steel to make the cut.

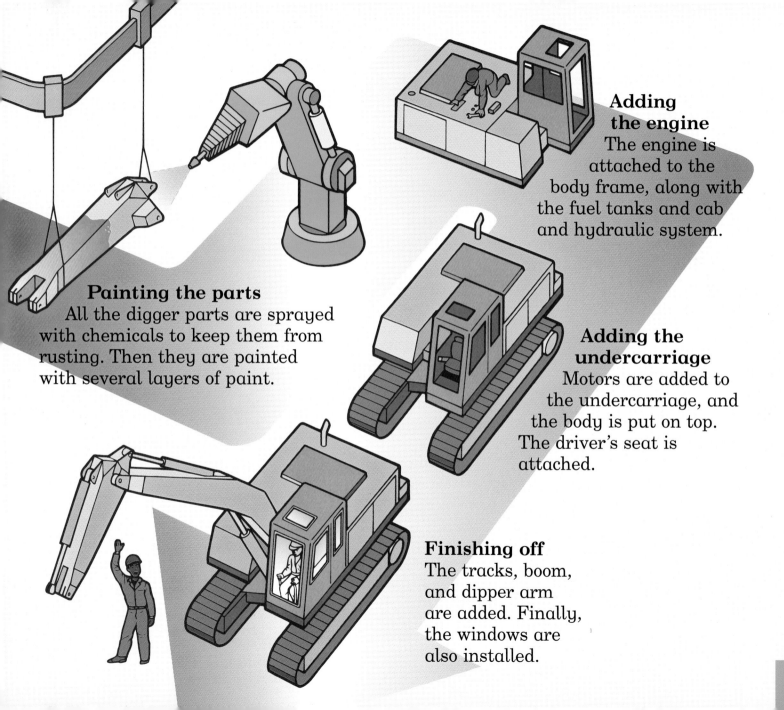

Painting the parts
All the digger parts are sprayed with chemicals to keep them from rusting. Then they are painted with several layers of paint.

Adding the engine
The engine is attached to the body frame, along with the fuel tanks and cab and hydraulic system.

Adding the undercarriage
Motors are added to the undercarriage, and the body is put on top. The driver's seat is attached.

Finishing off
The tracks, boom, and dipper arm are added. Finally, the windows are also installed.

Special Parts

⬤ The digger's bucket can be replaced with a different tool.

⬤ You can see some of the different tools here.

⬤ You can also see some tools that fit other types of diggers.

Grab

A grab is a huge claw that picks up scrap metal or logs. The grab is opened and closed by hydraulic rams. It hangs on the end of a very long boom.

Loading shovel

This shovel is used with a digger called a loader. It has a wide bucket for scooping up material.

Split bucket

Loaders also use a split bucket to move sand or gravel from one place to another. The bucket opens like a mouth and bites into the material.

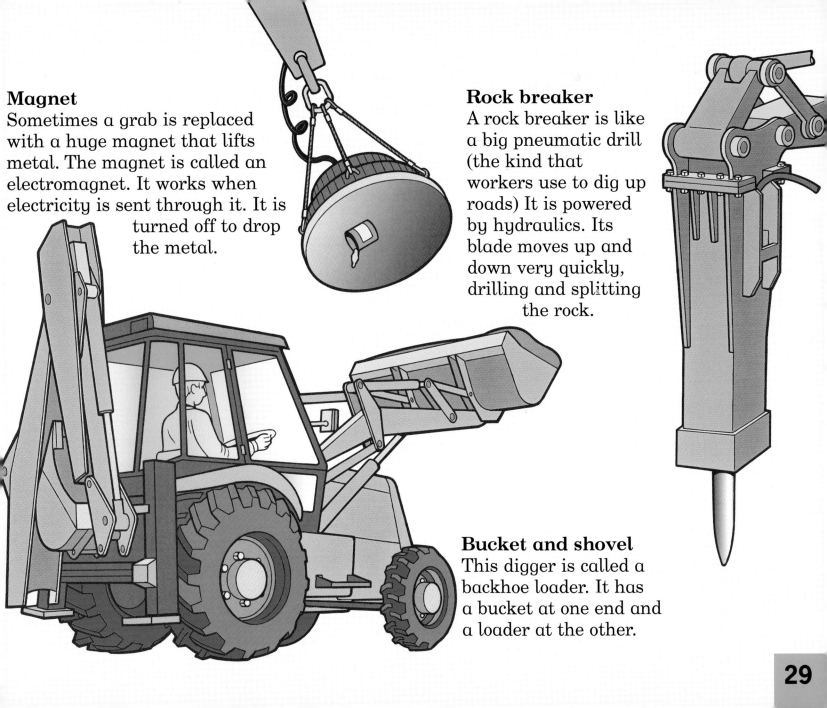

Magnet
Sometimes a grab is replaced with a huge magnet that lifts metal. The magnet is called an electromagnet. It works when electricity is sent through it. It is turned off to drop the metal.

Rock breaker
A rock breaker is like a big pneumatic drill (the kind that workers use to dig up roads) It is powered by hydraulics. Its blade moves up and down very quickly, drilling and splitting the rock.

Bucket and shovel
This digger is called a backhoe loader. It has a bucket at one end and a loader at the other.

Useful Words

backhoe excavator
A digger that has one arm for digging into the ground. The digger in this book is a backhoe excavator.

bearing A part of a machine that holds a moving part and lets it move easily.

boom The part of a digger's arm that is connected to its body. The dipper arm is connected to the other end.

bucket The scoop on the end of a digger's arm that breaks and picks up rocks and soil.

clamp A device that holds something firmly in place. Clamps hold hydraulic pipes in place on a digger.

crankshaft The part of an engine that is turned by the engine's pistons moving up and down.

cylinder A tube inside which a piston moves up and down. A digger has cylinders in its engine as well as cylinders that are part of its hydraulic rams.

dipper arm The part of a digger's arm that hangs on the end of the boom. The bucket is attached to the end of the dipper arm.

gear wheel A wheel with teeth around the outside. When two gear wheels are put together, turning one wheel makes the other wheel turn, too.

grab A tool that a digger can use to pick up logs or scrap metal.

hydraulic A hydraulic machine works when fluid is pumped into it. A digger's hydraulic system moves all its parts.

hydraulic motor An engine that turns when hydraulic fluid is pumped into it. A digger's tracks are moved by hydraulic motors.

hydraulic pipe A strong metal or rubber pipe carrying hydraulic fluid around the digger's hydraulic system.

loading shovel A wide bucket used for picking up and moving huge amounts of sand or soil.

outrigger A leg that sticks out of the side of a wheeled digger. Two outriggers keep the digger steady when it is working.

piston A part that moves up and down inside a cylinder. A digger has pistons in its engine and in its hydraulic rams.

pneumatic A pneumatic machine works when air is pumped into it. A road drill is a pneumatic machine.

ram A cylinder with a piston inside it. Hydraulic fluid makes the piston move in or out. Rams make the part of a digger's arm move.

rock breaker A very powerful drill that can be attached to a digger's arm. It can break rocks or concrete.

swing motor The hydraulic motor in a digger that makes the digger's body swing around while its undercarriage stays still.

track A long, wide loop of metal that moves around. A digger has two tracks that keep it from sinking into mud and move it along on soft ground.

undercarriage The bottom part of a digger that touches the ground. The undercarriage stays still while the body moves around. Some diggers have a tracked undercarriage, and some have a wheeled undercarriage.

ventilation system The parts of a digger's body that make sure that there is always fresh air inside the digger's cab.

Index